NOV 2011

ED

Cool

CAKE & CUPCAKE FOOD ART

Easy Recipes That Make Food Fun to Eat!

Nancy Tuminelly

ABDO
Publishing Company

To Adult Helpers

This is not your ordinary cookbook! Sure, we've provided ingredients lists and how-to photographs. But like any artistic endeavor, food art is all about creativity! Encourage kids to come up with their own ideas. Get creative with ingredients too. Scan your fridge and get started with whatever you have!

Always supervise kids when they are working in the kitchen. Food art often requires a lot of knife work such as slicing and shaping. Assist young artists whenever they are using knives. Occasionally, kids will need to use the oven or stovetop too. Be there to help when necessary, but encourage them to do as much as they can on their own. Kids love to share and eat their own creations!

Expect your young food artists to make a mess, but also expect them to clean up after themselves. Show them how to properly store unused ingredients. Most importantly, be a voice of encouragement. You might even get kids to eat healthy foods they've never had before!

Visit us at www.abdopublishing.com

Published by ABDO Publishing Company, 8000 West 78th Street, Edina, Minnesota 55439. Copyright © 2011 by Abdo Consulting Group, Inc. International copyrights reserved in all countries. No part of this book may be reproduced in any form without written permission from the publisher. Checkerboard Library™ is a trademark and logo of ABDO Publishing Company.

Printed in the United States of America, North Mankato, Minnesota
062010
092010

♻ PRINTED ON RECYCLED PAPER

Editor: Liz Salzmann
Series Concept: Nancy Tuminelly
Cover and Interior Design: Anders Hanson, Mighty Media, Inc.
Photo Credits: Anders Hanson, Shutterstock, iStock Photo

The following manufacturers/names appearing in this book are trademarks: Baker's Angel Flake brand, Cake Mate®, India Tree, Pillsbury® Creamy Supreme®, Wilton® Decorating Icing®

Library of Congress Cataloging-in-Publication Data

Tuminelly, Nancy, 1952-
  Cool cake & cupcake food art : easy recipes that make food fun to eat! / Nancy Tuminelly.
    p. cm. -- (Cool food art)
  Includes index.
  ISBN 978-1-61613-362-7
  1. Cake--Juvenile literature. 2. Cupcakes--Juvenile literature. 3. Food presentation--Juvenile literature. I. Title.
  TX771.T793 2011
  641.8'653--dc22
                        2010003287

CONTENTS

PAGE 14

PAGE 22

PAGE 24

PAGE 26

PLAY WITH YOUR FOOD!

Unless Mom says not to!

It's time to play with your food! Get ready to make funny faces, golf greens, and chocolate pandas! You're an artist now. The plate is your **canvas**, and your favorite foods are your paints!

As you make your cool cake and cupcake food art, be open to all sorts of ingredients. You can use anything! Candy pieces, icing, and sprinkles work really well. You can use them to create just about any **design**! Use ingredients that you like, but don't be afraid to try new things.

Like any kind of art, food art is about **expression** and creativity. Get inspired and give each dessert your own special touch. A lot of cookbooks teach you how to make food that tastes great. This book will inspire you to make cakes and cupcakes that taste and look great!

THE BASICS

Get started with a few important basics

ASK PERMISSION

> Before you cook, get permission to use the kitchen, cooking tools, and ingredients.

> You might want an adult to help you with some of your creations. But if you want to do something yourself, say so!

> When you need help, just ask. An adult should always be around when you are using sharp knives, the oven, or the stove.

BE PREPARED

> Read through the recipe before you begin.

> Get organized. Have your tools and ingredients ready before you start.

> Think of **alternative** ingredients if you want!

BE SMART, BE SAFE

> Never work in the kitchen when you are home alone!

> Always use sharp tools with care. Have an adult nearby when you are using a knife. Use a cutting board when you are working with a knife.

> Work slowly and carefully. Great food art rarely happens when you rush!

> An adult should always be around when you are using the oven.

BE NEAT AND CLEAN

> Start with clean hands, clean tools, and a clean work surface.

> Tie back long hair so it stays out of the way and out of the food!

> Wear comfortable clothes that can get a little bit dirty. Roll up your sleeves.

SAVING INGREDIENTS

When you are making food art, sometimes you only need a little bit of something. That means you have to do a good job of putting things away so they stay fresh. Cover leftover ingredients so that they will keep. Airtight containers work best. You don't want to waste a lot of food!

Note on Ingredients

The recipes in this book provide suggestions. Feel free to be creative! For example, a recipe may call for flaked coconut. Do you like coconut? Then add more! If you don't like coconut, then try something else!

KEY SYMBOLS

In this book, you will see some symbols beside the recipes. Here is what they mean.

Sharp!

You need to use a knife for this recipe. Ask an adult to stand by.

Hot!

This activity requires the use of an oven or stove. You need adult supervision. Always use oven mitts when holding hot pans.

THE COOLEST

CAKE MIX

FROSTING

ICING

SMALL CANDY PIECES

SPRINKLES

COLORED SUGAR CRYSTALS

PULL AND PEEL LICORICE

FRUIT LEATHER ROLLS

CANDY SPEARMINTS

INGREDIENTS

CHOCOLATE-COVERED
PRETZEL STICKS

PRETZEL STICKS

CHOCOLATE-COVERED
PRETZEL ROUNDS

SMALL PRETZELS

FLAKED COCONUT

GRAHAM CRACKERS

MARSHMALLOWS

MINI MARSHMALLOWS

FOOD COLORING

THE TOOL BOX

Here are some tools you'll need for most food art recipes

PARING KNIFE

TOOTHPICKS

ICING TIPS

BREAD KNIFE

SMALL SPATULA

MEASURING CUPS
AND SPOONS

BOWLS

CUTTING BOARD

TECHNIQUES

Tips for making great food art

BAKING CAKES AND CUPCAKES

You can make cake batter from scratch. But it's much easier to buy box mixes. Usually, all you have to do is add water, eggs, and oil! The directions on the box will tell you how to bake the cake or cupcakes. If you follow the directions, your treats will turn out great!

No Sticking Allowed!

Grease the pan before you add the batter. Butter wrappers work great. Or you can use waxed paper and a bit of butter. Rub the butter all around the inside of the pan. If you're making cupcakes, you can use paper or foil liners instead.

Are They Done Yet?

All ovens are a little bit different, so watch the edges of your treats as they bake. When they're done, the edges will start to pull away from the pan. Stick a toothpick into the center. If it comes out clean, your treats are done! Cakes usually need to bake longer than cupcakes.

Cooling Your Treats

When the baking is done, put the pan on a cooling rack. After about five minutes, remove the cake or cupcakes from the pan. Always let cakes and cupcakes cool completely before frosting them.

WORKING WITH FROSTING

Applying frosting is an art! Make sure the cake is completely cool before you start. Stir the frosting very well, especially if you are combining two frostings or adding food coloring. The more you stir, the smoother and creamier the frosting becomes.

Use a spatula or dinner knife. Make sure you have plenty of frosting on the utensil. Then carefully spread the frosting onto the treats. Make it as smooth as you can.

APPLYING ICING

With icing, the possibilities are endless! There are many color choices. There are also many different icing tips that you can use. Each one makes a different **design**. Here are some icing tips and what they do!

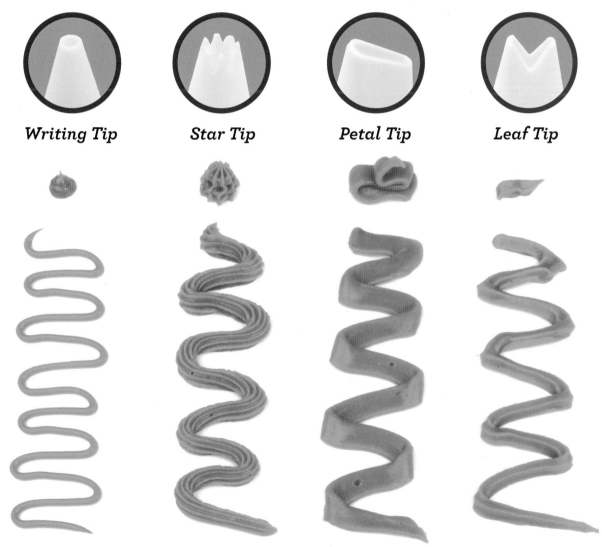

Writing Tip **Star Tip** **Petal Tip** **Leaf Tip**

PLAY BALL
CUPCAKES

Nobody will call a foul on these sporty cakes!

INGREDIENTS

1 cupcake

white frosting

pull and peel licorice

red icing

red and yellow sugar crystals

TOOLS

dinner knife

cutting board

paring knife

icing tips

Baseball

1 Cover the cupcake with white frosting.

2 Cut two strips of pull and peel licorice. Place them on the frosting. These are the baseball's **seams**.

3 Use red icing to make short lines across the licorice. This is the stitching.

4 Add some red and yellow sugar crystals to give the baseball a little more color.

MORE SPORTS

Don't play baseball? Try making these other sporty cupcakes!

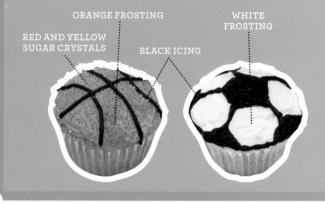

ORANGE FROSTING

WHITE FROSTING

RED AND YELLOW SUGAR CRYSTALS

BLACK ICING

FLOWER GARDEN
CAKE

More flower power than a pound of posies!

INGREDIENTS

9 x 13-inch cake

white frosting

food coloring

3 mini cupcakes

colored sugar
crystals

sprinkles

colored icing

fruit leather

candy
spearmints

TOOLS

platter

bowls

measuring cups
& spoons

small spatula

dinner knife

fork

icing tips

1 Set the cake on a **platter**. Put about 1⅓ cups of white frosting in a bowl. Stir in a few drops of blue food coloring. Keep adding food coloring until the frosting is the color of the sky. Frost the top and sides of the cake.

2 Stir green food coloring into the remaining blue frosting. Keep adding food coloring until it is the color of grass. Spread it over the bottom end of the cake.

3 Use food coloring to make colored frosting for the flowers. Make 2 tablespoons of frosting for each cupcake. Frost the mini cupcakes. Then add colored sugar crystals and sprinkles.

4 Place the mini cupcakes on the cake.

5 Make the flower petals with colored icing. Roll up thin pieces of green fruit leather for stems. Add candy spearmints for leaves.

6 Use colored icing to draw the sun.

MAGNIFICENT
MONARCH

Eat your monarch before it migrates!

INGREDIENTS

1 8-inch round chocolate cake

1 chocolate cupcake

2 mini chocolate cupcakes

chocolate frosting

white frosting

red and yellow food coloring

black icing

4 mini marshmallows

small white sprinkles

chocolate-covered pretzel sticks

TOOLS

cutting board

bread knife

icing tips

butter knife

bowl

measuring cup

1 Place the cake on a cutting board. Cut the cake in half. Cut each half into a large piece and a small piece.

2 Cover all of the cupcakes with chocolate frosting. Arrange the cake pieces and cupcakes into the butterfly's wings and body (see page 18).

3 Put about 1 cup of white frosting in a bowl. Add red and yellow food coloring to make it orange. Stir in just a few drops at a time.

4 Spread the orange frosting on the cake pieces. Don't go all the way to the edges.

5 Outline the orange frosting with black icing. Use a large, writing icing tip. Then draw black lines on top of the orange icing.

6 Cut the mini marshmallows in half. Put two halves on the large cupcake for eyes. Put the rest of the marshmallow halves around the edges of the cake slices. Arrange some white sprinkles around the edges of the cake.

7 Put a few more white sprinkles on the large cupcake. **Insert** the chocolate covered pretzel sticks next to the eyes.

CUTE AS A BUG
CUPCAKES

This is one sweet and crunchy butterfly!

INGREDIENTS

1 chocolate cupcake

chocolate frosting

orange icing

pretzel stick

small candy piece

2 small pretzels

2 sprinkles

TOOLS

small spatula

icing tips

1 Cover the cupcake with chocolate frosting.

2 Put a petal tip on a tube of orange icing. Draw a flower-shaped border around the edge of the cupcake.

3 Break the pretzel stick in half. Place one half in the center of the cupcake. Put a small candy at one end of the pretzel stick.

4 Push the small pretzels into the frosting. Put one on each side of the pretzel stick. These are the butterfly's wings.

5 Place two small sprinkles next to the small candy for antennae.

PORTLY
PANDA

This panda is almost too cute to eat!

INGREDIENTS

2 chocolate cupcakes

white frosting

small candy piece

black icing

white sprinkles

2 chocolate-covered pretzel rounds

2 mini chocolate cupcakes

TOOLS

dinner knife

icing tips

plate

cutting board

bread knife

1 Cover both large cupcakes with white frosting.

2 Place a small candy in the center of one cupcake for a nose.

3 Use black icing to draw two curved shapes for the eyes. Place a white sprinkle on each eye for a **highlight**. Draw the mouth with black icing.

4 Put the chocolate-covered pretzel rounds above the eyes for ears.

5 Place the head on a plate. Place the second frosted cupcake below it for the body.

6 Cut the mini cupcakes in half. Stick three white sprinkles into the edge of each half. Arrange them around the body. They are the panda's arms and legs.

LET'S MONKEY AROUND!

Try a monkey version with these ingredients!

SPRINKLES

CHOCOLATE-COVERED PRETZEL ROUNDS

PULL AND PEEL LICORICE

PRETZEL STICKS

LET IT SNOW
CUPCAKES

This delicious snowman will warm your heart!

INGREDIENTS

1 chocolate cupcake

white frosting

2 marshmallows

1 pretzel stick

1 small orange candy
piece

7-inch strip of pull
and peel licorice

1 chocolate-covered
pretzel round

black icing

flaked coconut

TOOLS

butter knife

cutting board

paring knife

toothpick

icing tips

1 Cover the cupcake with white frosting.

2 Break the pretzel stick in half. Push the broken ends into opposite sides of a marshmallow.

3 Cut a little bit off the end of the other marshmallow to make it smaller than the body. Use a toothpick to make a hole in the side. Push a small orange candy nose into the hole.

4 Tie a loose knot in the licorice. Arrange the loop around the edge of the body. Put the head on top of the licorice. Use a little frosting to hold it in place.

5 Set the snowman in the middle of the frosted cupcake. Use a little frosting to **attach** the chocolate covered pretzel to the top of the snowman.

6 Use black icing to add eyes and buttons.

7 Set the cupcake on a plate. Sprinkle flaked coconut over the snowman and cupcake to make snow.

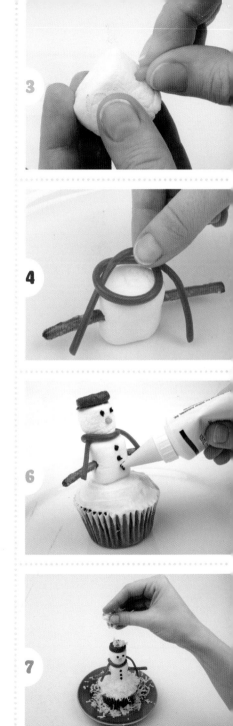

HOLE IN ONE
CUPCAKES

These treats break par every time!

INGREDIENTS

white frosting

green food coloring

2 white cupcakes

green sugar crystals

red fruit leather

1 crushed graham cracker

small candy pieces

pull and peel licorice

TOOLS

measuring cup

bowl

dinner knife

paring knife

cutting board

toothpicks

1 Put about ½ cup of white frosting in a bowl. Add green food coloring until the frosting is green. Stir in just a few drops at a time.

2 Cover the cupcakes with green frosting. Sprinkle a lot of green crystals on top.

3 Cut a diamond shape out of the red fruit leather. Wrap it around a toothpick to make a flag. Stick the flag into one of the cupcakes.

4 Place a small white candy next to the flag.

5 Pile the crushed graham cracker on the other cupcake. Make a dent in the crumbs with the side of your thumb to look like a sand trap.

6 Make a golf club. Stick a toothpick into a small candy. Wrap a strip of licorice around the other end. Set the club on one of the cupcakes.

CUPCAKE
CREW

Make a face for everyone in your crew!

INGREDIENTS

1 cupcake

white frosting

chocolate frosting

colored icing

small candy pieces

sprinkles

TOOLS

bowl

butter knife

icing tips

1 Put some white frosting in a bowl. Stir in chocolate frosting until the mixture is the skin color you want.

2 Cover the cupcake with frosting.

3 Make two ovals of white icing for the eyes. Place small candy pieces on top of the icing.

4 Use more small candy pieces to add a nose and rosy cheeks, if you like.

5 Draw the mouth with red or pink icing.

6 Add hair with colored icing or sprinkles.

WRAP IT UP!

Food art finale!

Now you're ready to **design** your own cakes and cupcakes! It helps to have a plan before you start. Make a quick **sketch** of your idea. Add notes about what ingredients might work best. Talk about your sketch with others. You will get great ideas! Make sure you take photographs before you eat your creations. The better your cakes and cupcakes look, the more likely they are to be eaten!

Cakes and cupcakes make great gifts. They are also great for **celebrating** special events such as birthdays and holidays. You could make a special cake for your mom or some sporty cupcakes for your coach. The more you experiment with food art, the more fun you can have!

GLOSSARY

ALTERNATIVE – different from the original.

ATTACH – to join two things together.

CANVAS – a type of thick cloth that artists paint on.

CELEBRATE – to honor with a party or special ceremony.

DESIGN – 1. a decorative pattern or arrangement. 2. to plan how something will appear or work.

EXPRESSION – creating a work of art as a way to show one's feelings.

HIGHLIGHT – a spot or streak that more light shines on, making it look a lighter color.

INSERT – to stick something into something else.

PLATTER – a large plate.

SEAM – the line where two edges meet.

SKETCH – a drawing.

Web Sites

To learn more about cool food art, visit ABDO Publishing Company on the World Wide Web at **www.abdopublishing.com.** Web sites about cool food art are featured on our Book Links page. These links are routinely monitored and updated to provide the most current information available.

INDEX